HOW TO HEAR FROM GOD

An Experiential Journey

Catherine Toon, MD

HOW TO HEAR FROM GOD
by Catherine Toon, MD

Published by Imprint Publishing
PO Box 63125 Colorado Springs, CO 80962-3125
United States
www.catherinetoon.com
Phone: (724) 677-6801
Email: info@catherinetoon.com

All rights reserved. This book or parts thereof may not be reproduced in any form, stored in a retrieval system, or transmitted in any form by any means electronic, mechanical, photocopy, recording, or otherwise without prior written permission of the publisher, except as provided by United States of America copyright law.

Copyright © 2020 by Catherine Toon
All rights reserved.

ISBN: 978-0-9995910-8-6 (Paperback Edition)
ISBN: 978-0-9995910-3-1 (Electronic Edition)

Library of Congress Control Number - 2020906754
Printed in the United States of America
First Printing 2020

Credits and Permissions:
Scripture taken from the Holy Bible, NEW INTERNATIONAL VERSION, NIV. Copyright 1973, 1978, 1984, 2011 by Biblica, Inc. Used by permission. All rights reserved worldwide.

Scripture quotations taken from the New American Standard Bible (NASB), Copyright 1960, 1962, 1963, 1968, 1971, 1972, 1973, 1975, 1977, 1995 by The Lockman Foundation. Used by permission. www.Lockman.org

Scripture quotations taken from the Amplified Bible (AMP), Copyright 2015 by The Lockman Foundation. Used by permission. www.Lockman.org

Verses listed without translation references are partially quoted or inferred Scripture quotations taken from the Amplified Bible (AMPC), Copyright 1954, 1958, 1962, 1964, 1965, 1987 by The Lockman Foundation. Used by permission. www.Lockman.org

Scripture taken from the New King James Version. Copyright 1982 by Thomas Nelson. Used by permission. All rights reserved.

Scripture quotations marked TPT are from The Passion Translation®. Copyright © 2017, 2018 by Passion & Fire Ministries, Inc. Used by permission. All rights reserved. ThePassionTranslation.com.

All Scripture quotations are from The Passion Translation®. Copyright © 2017, 2018 by Passion & Fire Ministries, Inc. Used by permission. All rights reserved. ThePassionTranslation.com.

Scripture taken from the King James Bible is Public domain and may be used freely, without restriction and without prior permission.

Scripture quotations are taken from the Holy Bible, New Living Translation, copyright 1996, 2004, 2007, 2013, 2015 by Tyndale House Foundation. Used by permission of Tyndale House Publishers, Inc., Carol Stream, Illinois 60188. All rights reserved.

Scripture quotations marked (TLB) are taken from The Living Bible copyright 1971. Used by permission of Tyndale House Publishers, Inc., Carol Stream, Illinois 60188. All rights reserved.

Book Cover by Gwendolyn Enlow; Interior Design by hamanutdesign.com; Graphics & Photography by Thrive VIP, LLC; Photography by Jess Henderson and Drew Wilbur; Compilation by Allison Jackson; Editing by Sarah Watne, Rachel Toon, and Becky Royer

WHAT OTHER MINISTERS ARE SAYING ABOUT CATHERINE

~~~

"Catherine Toon is a powerhouse of peace. The reflection of Jesus that shines through her and her ministry brings healing to the deepest places in hearts. You simply can't be around her without feeling the Father's perfect love. Her prophetic teaching, coaching, and healing gifts stream from the overflow of her own personal transformation and encounters with the One who loves you unconditionally and completely. You'll leave her presence knowing that you are absolutely loved, believed in, and empowered to be exactly who God created you to be."

Schlyce Jimenez (Founder of Emerge School of Transformation)

"Catherine Toon reminds me of a mixture between the skilled surgeon that knows exactly what needs to happen to bring wholeness, mixed with the nurses that ensure you that everything is going to be ok when you're getting your first set of shots as a little boy or girl. She carries such an incredible authority, but truly operates in it to serve those people she has been entrusted with."

Justin Knapp (Senior Leader at Pulse)

"It is with high regard and sincere humility that I have the privilege of endorsing Catherine. I have known Catherine for over three years. I have monthly been a part of her life, development, growth, and training. I have never met another person more capable to do the ministry God has called her to do. Capable in character and integrity. She has served and submitted herself to a growth (death to herself) process that few would endure. She has allowed the Lord to fashion in her His character of humility, loyalty, kindness, purity, faithfulness, genuine beauty - in essence, the fruit of the spirit with a heart to serve and give to others more than she receives. Capable in giftedness and ability. Catherine's ability to mix the prophetic gifts she possesses (you could stop right here) with her mastery of the supernatural mind renewal prayer process is a powerful ministry of freedom and the binding of broken hearts. Capable in relationships. Catherine is proven in relationships. An honoring wife, a loved mother, an elder in the church, and a leader of leaders. I unreservedly recommend the person Catherine Toon and in so doing can also recommend the ministry that flows out of the genuineness of a life conformed to the character and image of our Lord Jesus Christ."

Nathan Blouse, Apostle, Pastor (Safe Place Ministries)

"Catherine Toon has been an amazing blessing to me and my family. She humbly flows in the prophetic, but with great accuracy. She literally prophesied something to me one day and it happened the next day just like she said. I was really amazed, but I was more comforted by the fact that I have a voice like hers in my life."

Pastor Joe Barlow, President/Founder (Joseph Barlow Ministries)

"Catherine Toon is more than an author and speaker. Catherine is a gift to this generation. Her ability to articulate truth is both refreshing and inspiring. If you want your world rocked and challenged for the better, I highly recommend her. Rarely will you find communicators who are both dynamic and clear - with her, you get both."

Myron Pierce, Lead Pastor (Mission Church)

"Dr. Catherine Toon is a prophetic voice speaking to us from the heart of the Father. She communicates truth in love and enables you to see yourself in Christ. Catherine has a great desire to see others walk in wholeness and the awareness of unity. Her words are both powerful and inspirational. Her voice creates an atmosphere of love that is contagious. My encounters with Catherine have always left me with the awareness that I am loved and the experience of being in His tangible presence. It is an honor to call her my friend. I would highly recommend Catherine to anyone seeking the voice of Christ."

Michael Porter, Founder (Love University); Instructor (World Bible School University); CEO (Signet Management Group Inc.)

I pray that the Father of glory, the God of our Lord Jesus Christ, would impart to you the riches of the Spirit of wisdom and the Spirit of revelation to know him through your deepening intimacy with him.

Ephesians 1:17 (TPT)

CONTENTS

12	INTRODUCTION
13	YOUR FIVE SPIRITUAL SENSES
14	WHY IS CONNECTING WITH GOD SO IMPORTANT?
16	DIFFERENT WAYS OF CONNECTING WITH GOD
18	YOUR FIVE SPIRITUAL SENSES
30	FEELING THE HEART OF GOD
34	GOD THINKING THROUGH YOU
36	KNOWING IN YOUR "KNOWER"
38	BEING LED THROUGH SCRIPTURE
40	BEING LED THROUGH SUPERNATURAL SIGNS
44	HOW TO KNOW WHEN YOU ARE HEARING GOD
48	WHAT DOES LOVE LOOK LIKE?
50	SUBMITTING WHAT YOU'RE GETTING
52	PRACTICING CONNECTING WITH GOD
54	GROWING IN YOUR CONNECTION
56	IT'S OK TO MISS IT
58	IMPARTATION
60	ABOUT CATHERINE
62	SHARE YOUR TESTIMONY
63	CONNECT WITH CATHERINE
64	FOLLOW
65	REQUEST
66	RESOURCES

INTRODUCTION

~~~

Do you want a renewed passion to connect with and "hear" from God for yourself? Do you want to discover your unique way of "hearing" Him? Even if this is something you've been operating in for a long time, it's not uncommon to feel distance, grow too familiar with His voice, or lose a little bit of your awe and excitement in this area. Our ability to connect with Him is so valuable and precious that it behooves us to always cultivate, practice, and grow in this area.

For those of you who want a renewed appreciation or just some practical help for hearing from the Lord at a higher level, keep reading. I have put this together just for you! There is always a deeper experiential connection that the Lord wants with you. You are the object of His passion!

We never leave the simplicity of the Gospel that secured our intimacy with God, we just delve deeper and deeper into its encompassing goodness. That's true about our ability to connect with and experience God as well. We are always invited to go deeper with Him. God wants to be known. He speaks and wants to be heard; and He has given you the inherent capacity to connect with Him more and more on an experiential level. That is so amazing!

Chapter 1

WHY IS CONNECTING WITH GOD SO IMPORTANT?

~~~

When I am ministering to people, I often hear that they really struggle with hearing God. This can be a place of torment. It definitely does not have to be this way! You were made for connection with Him. You were made to experience Him intimately. When you connect with God, peace comes. That's when answers come. That's when your faith is able to rise and when your heart is healed. Intimate relationship with God and the awareness of that connection is what makes real life come into your being. That's when the Word becomes flesh.

Your intimacy with God is all about connection. You are one with a God Who is intimately, perpetually, and passionately in love with you. If you are not experiencing this reality, then there's a breakdown in your connection.

It is your birthright to experience God - to experience who He is for you and to experience who you are in Him. He wants you to connect with Him on an experiential level because He is Love

(1 John 4:8,16), and Love transforms us! The Word of God says that when we see Him, as in a mirror, we are transformed from glory to glory (2 Corinthians 3:18, TPT):

We can all draw close to him with the veil removed from our faces. And with no veil we all become like mirrors who brightly reflect the glory of the Lord Jesus. We are being transfigured into his very image as we move from one brighter level of glory to another. And this glorious transfiguration comes from the Lord, who is the Spirit.

Chapter 2

DIFFERENT WAYS OF CONNECTING WITH GOD

~~~

God designed every one of us for connection. You are wired for connection. You are also an individual, wired in a specific and unique way. Your way of receiving from God is as unique as your relationship with Him. Not everyone "hears God" in the same way. One mode of "hearing" is not more important or desirable than another.

When you walk as one spirit with the Lord (1 Corinthians 6:17), He uses the faintest whisper, image, or thought to get your attention. He is a master communicator and knows exactly the best way to connect with you, His beloved - the object of His passion. Usually, there is a primary way that He uses most often with you because of the way you are wired. Let's look at some of the ways He connects with us.

Chapter 3

YOUR FIVE SPIRITUAL SENSES

~~~

Everyone has five spiritual senses that parallel with the five natural senses. You may not be aware of them, but you have them right now! Seeing, hearing, tasting, smelling, and feeling are senses that you have in both the physical and spiritual realms. You can see in the spirit, hear in the spirit, and taste, smell and feel in the spirit. Once you awaken to Christ in you, your spirit (the real you) can experience your oneness with Him all the time.

In Ephesians, Paul prayed for the believers at the Church of Ephesus, that the eyes of their heart would be opened (Ephesians 1:18, AMP):

And [I pray] that the eyes of your heart [the very center and core of your being] may be enlightened [flooded with light by the Holy Spirit], so that you will know and cherish the hope [the divine guarantee, the confident expectation] to which He has called you, the riches of His glorious inheritance in the saints (God's people)

This is about awakening your spiritual senses. The Spirit of Wisdom and Revelation needs to stir up or awaken your senses, so that you can know and experience the hope of His calling, the glories of the riches of the inheritance in the saints, and His mighty power towards you.

The "eyes of your heart" refer to how you see in your imagination. Some translations bring this understanding out. However, many of us tend to be dull to the things of the Spirit. There's no condemnation with this! It is helpful to honestly observe how sharp our senses are so that we can ask for our Helper to come awaken our awareness and fine-tune our senses. The great news is that God desires to awaken your spiritual senses even more than you want Him to! He longs to connect with you experientially every day, all the time.

So, let's unpack each of our spiritual senses. If you desire to have your spiritual senses awakened in a greater fashion so you can connect with God, receive this prayer over you:

Papa,

I thank You that You love Your kids so much that You want them close. You desire that they would know Your heart for them. You want them to know who You have made them to be, specifically and uniquely. I thank You for jumping off these pages and for being tangible to each and every person right where and how they need it. I thank You for enlightening the eyes of their imaginations and for all Your kids' spiritual senses to be awakened, heightened, and trained in discernment. I thank You that Your perspectives will be revealed and only Your agendas will be accomplished. I thank You, Holy Spirit, for leading each and every person into the Truth of Who You, Jesus, and Holy Spirit are as Love. I thank You for heaven invading earth right here, right now, right where each and every person is. I thank You for Your fruit abounding. I thank You for power released in Your Love and that each and every person will walk away beautifully and powerfully transformed. I give You all the glory and honor and praise, because You truly rock! In Jesus' name, amen!

Seeing

It is possible for us to see in the spiritual realm and the physical realm. In 2 Kings 6:17, Elisha prayed that his servant's eyes would be opened so that he could see what was going on in the spirit realm.

And Elisha prayed, "Open his eyes, Lord, so that he may see." Then the Lord opened the servant's eyes, and he looked and saw the hills full of horses and chariots of fire all around Elisha.

After Elisha's servant's spiritual eyes were opened, he could see spiritually and physically. The Bible is full of examples of people seeing with their spiritual eyes. You also have the ability to connect with God in this way!

God did this for me when Robert, my son who struggles with autism, was a little, little boy. My mother was watching my three children as my husband and I were on a little mini-moon, hiking. We came down the mountain and when we regained cell service, I heard a panicked message from my mom. Robert was gone! Fear grabbed me by the throat as I began to pray in the Spirit, releasing angels over him. Suddenly, God showed me this in the Spirit:

Robert was in a green golf shirt and underwear. He was barefoot and running down a side street toward a busy intersection near our home. There was this HUGE angel running right by his side – smiling, as if they were out for a happy jaunt.

I listened to the next message my mom left. WHEW – crisis averted. The police called my mom and explained they had Robert. They were bringing him home. A kind woman had stopped her car as Robert crossed the busy intersection and stayed with him as she called the police at the same time my mom had. Robert said he was looking for his dad.

After the crisis, I asked my mother what he was wearing and what intersection he was found at. She said that he was wearing a green golf shirt and underwear and that he was barefoot. He was found at the busy intersection I had seen him running towards with the angel. Connecting in the Spirit can save lives!

God uses images and moving pictures in our imagination to communicate to us. You may be praying for someone and see an image of their brain or heart or some other part of their body. This may be the Lord encouraging you to pray for healing in that area. You may see an image of a broken heart and know that the Lord wants to minister to their broken heart.

Early on when I was first learning how to "see in the Spirit," I was praying for someone who had just brought her son to the hospital. She asked me to pray, but didn't tell me what to pray for. As I prayed, God showed me a kidney. So, I released healing into the son's kidneys. My prayer was short and had no "zing" to it. I honestly forgot about it, until 2 weeks later, she found me and excitedly told me her son's kidneys were healed! God wants to partner with YOU in this and many other ways as well - He is not respecter of persons (Romans 2:11)!

The Lord also uses visions and dreams to communicate with us. Many times, when you have a picture, vision, or dream, you will want to ask the Lord for interpretation. Ask Him what He's showing you. He will start to unpack and expand what He showed you. In Jeremiah 1:11-12 (NIV), we see how the Lord explains the meaning of what He showed the prophet Jeremiah.

¹¹ The word of the Lord came to me: "What do you see, Jeremiah?" "I see the branch of an almond tree," I replied.
¹² The Lord said to me, "You have seen correctly, for I am watching to see that my word is fulfilled."

Everything God speaks contains an invitation for Him to speak even more and give meaning. God may also give you instruction or direction through a vision like He did with Paul when he directed him to preach in Macedonia (Acts 16:9-10, NIV):

⁹ During the night Paul had a vision of a man of Macedonia standing and begging him, "Come over to Macedonia and help us." 10 After Paul had seen the vision, we got ready at once to leave for Macedonia, concluding that God had called us to preach the gospel to them.

If this is the primary way you connect to God, what you receive will be visual more often than not. However, if you have never experienced this, relax. It is probably not your primary way of receiving. HOWEVER, you can develop your spiritual sense of seeing - as you can any of your spiritual senses. Share your desire with Holy Spirit, relax, turn your attention to Him, and let Him lead. As you practice, He will do just that. Remember, He IS the word and you are His child – surely, He wants to communicate with you! Let's continue to the next way of connecting with God.

Hearing

When our spiritual ears are open, we can hear in several ways. God can communicate in an audible voice, but usually He usually speaks more subtly with an inner voice. After all He is inside you!

However, there are times when God does speak audibly, with a sound or voice that you actually hear with your physical ears. Some people have heard angels singing or have been awoken by their name being called. John 12:28-30 (NKJV) is a fascinating passage that not only illustrates God speaking audibly, but our difficulty in receiving this way:

⁸ Father, glorify Your name."
Then a voice came from heaven, saying, "I have both glorified it and will glorify it again."
²⁹ Therefore the people who stood by and heard it said that it had thundered. Others said, "An angel has spoken to Him."
³⁰ Jesus answered and said, "This voice did not come because of Me, but for your sake."
(Emphasis added)

Here, we see that when God spoke, some people thought it was an angel while others thought it was just thunder. God has rarely spoken audibly to me. One of the most precious moments for me is when I found out I was pregnant with my son, Robert. I laid back on the bed just praising God for my boy (I knew my baby was a boy). And I heard audibly in my left ear, "This one will be a preacher!"

I believe that God knew I needed something to war with that carried more weight than other prophetic words, because of the battles we would face with autism later. We can use what we hear from God to stand against the things that come against us (1 Timothy 1:18).

We can make mistakes with what we think we are getting from God. I can't resist sharing one of mine that just recently happened with "audible heavenly music". This just makes me laugh!

I was in my bathroom getting ready for the day and, suddenly,

I heard faint music. It was winter and I thought it sounded like the ice cream truck. That didn't make sense. It kept on going, so I went around the house investigating. It was localized to one side of the house. Here, not there...and so on. I started talking to the Lord, "Is this heavenly"? And I didn't hear Him say anything. Finally, after about 20 minutes, I realized it was coming from my phone in my bathroom. Why it started playing, and why on that particular music, I have no idea. It wasn't a special message from heaven, it was my phone! Papa/Jesus/Holy Spirit and I did have a good laugh, though! So, relax with all this!

But, with that, use this example to make sure you are not making something supernatural that just isn't. People (including myself in the past) have used their giftings to prop up insecurities when, instead, we need to get our self-worth and security from resting in God, Who adores us personally. Of course, God wants to minister to you personally. That is why I am sharing some experiences – to help stir your faith and appetite to experience for yourself. God is a good God with no favorites, but instead of trumping something up, we need to let Him "speak to us" in His own way.

Moving on, God also speaks in an inner audible voice. This sounds just like an audible voice except it comes from within you. It is stronger and clearer than a thought. It is a clear and distinct voice, but only audible to you and not those around you. Often it sounds like you, because it is Holy Spirit speaking through your spirit.

A cool example of this inner voice is when I lost my wedding ring. I turned the house upside down. I even hired someone with a metal detector to survey a dog park where I might have lost it. No ring. But the Lord had assured me I would find it. So, I tried to settle down my upset, but it was not fun. This went on for three months. Then, one morning, the Lord woke me up and said (in an inner audible voice), "Look in your sock drawer." I did.

And, behold, mystically, in the left corner of my overstuffed sock drawer (that I visited every day), was a clearing and in the middle of the clearing was my ring. How it got there, I have no clue, but I wasn't asking questions... I was just rejoicing!

God can be subtle and speak in a "still small voice" (1 Kings 19:11-13). This has a different feel to it than God thinking through you (the mind of Christ, 1 Corinthians 2:16). It is one thing to have an internal conversation and another to have a thought that didn't originate from you. I will discuss this more in Chapter 5 - God Thinking through You.

Hearing God on the inside is cultivated in the same fashion as all the other modalities – practice. He truly speaks and wants you to hear. Ideally, He wants to converse with you back and forth. Let's go on to some of the less common, but very real modalities.

Tasting

Have you ever walked away from a particular environment and thought to yourself, Yuck, that just left a bad taste in my mouth? You didn't physically taste anything, but spiritually you tasted something unpleasant. In contrast, you may have experienced a sweet time of worshipping Jesus, and when it was done you thought I love the taste of that! Psalm 34:8 tells us "Taste and see that the Lord is good." We do not physically taste God, but we do spiritually. You can learn to discern the sweet taste of the Lord's presence. His Word has a sweet taste as well (Psalm 119:103, NKJV).

[103] *How sweet are Your words to my taste, Sweeter than honey to my mouth!*

The Lord can also give you a specific taste that will help you discern a situation. Maybe a certain taste means something to you, so when the Lord puts that taste in your mouth, you know exactly what is going on. Your spiritual sense of taste can help you discern good and evil.

Smelling

You can also smell in the spiritual realm. You may be in a beautiful worship experience and smell the sweet aroma of the Lord's presence. Or, you may be praying for someone and begin to smell something that gives you revelation of how to minister to that person.

I remember one time when I was just enjoying God's sweet presence, I kept smelling what was kind of like roses. It grew stronger and stronger. Finally, I got up and hunted around to make sure there were no flowers, room freshener, etc. I saw Jesus smiling and then He "vanished"! The Bible says that God diffuses through us the fragrance of His knowledge (2 Corinthians 2:14, NKJV).

[14] Now thanks be to God who always leads us in triumph in Christ, and through us diffuses the fragrance of His knowledge in every place.

The finished work of Jesus on your life is a sweet smell to God (Ephesians 5:2, TPT)!

[2] And continue to walk surrendered to the extravagant love of Christ, for he surrendered his life as a sacrifice for us. His great love for us was pleasing to God, like an aroma of adoration—a sweet healing fragrance.

In the book of Philippians, Paul told those in Philippi that their sacrifice had a sweet smell (Philippians 4:18, TPT):

[18] I now have all I need—more than enough—I'm abundantly sat-

isfied! For I've received the gift you sent by Epaphroditus and viewed it as a sweet sacrifice, perfumed with the fragrance of your faithfulness, which is so pleasing to God!

Our spiritual sense of smell can help us discern a situation. If you begin smelling something that doesn't have a physical source, ask the Lord to give you understanding of what He is showing you.

Feeling or Touching

You can also be touched with things from the spiritual realm. You may sense a weightiness or electricity from the heavenly dimension. Perhaps you have felt the wind blow when there was no physical breeze and perceived that an angel was present. Or perhaps you have felt a hand rest on your shoulder when no one was there and felt encouraged knowing the Lord was there with you. Sometimes, there is a sensation of heat or of non-painful electricity.

During a spiritual encounter, the prophet Isaiah was touched by a coal from the altar (Isaiah 6:6-7, TPT):

6 Then out of the smoke, one of the angels of fire flew to me. He had in his hands a burning coal he had taken from the altar with tongs. 7 He touched my lips with it and said, "See? The burning coal from the altar has touched your lips. Your guilt is taken away; your sin is blotted out."

The prophet Jeremiah was touched by the hand of the Lord (Jeremiah 1:9, NIV).

9 Then the Lord reached out his hand and touched my mouth and said to me, "I have put my words in your mouth."

Another example of the spiritual sense if feeling is what is known as being "slain in the Spirit." This is a term for when the presence of God is so weighty that you literally can't stand or function (1 Kings 8:10-12). My personal favorite example of this in scripture (humor in the midst of the terrible seriousness with Jesus being arrested before He was crucified) is John 18:4-6 (NIV):

⁴ Jesus, knowing all that was going to happen to him, went out and asked them, "Who is it you want?"
⁵ "Jesus of Nazareth," they replied.
"I am he," Jesus said. (And Judas the traitor was standing there with them.) ⁶ When Jesus said, "I am he," they drew back and fell to the ground.

The first time this happened to me, personally, I was a young believer. I was in a Nazarene Church that didn't traditionally believe in/promote such things. I was being prayed for and I felt this intense, but glorious heaviness that seemed to push me backwards and down. I halfway glared at the woman thinking, "Why are you pushing me down?", but she was only holding my hands. She said, "It's OK" and, with that, down I went, in ecstatic glory! I felt God's heavy loving, indescribable weight, and electricity that stimulated, but didn't hurt. I wanted to stay there forever.

God's glory will affect your body – of course, because we are finite beings beholding and encountering an infinite God. When a gazillion watts of God works through a 3-amp fuse human, things are likely to get wonky! But it is worth it. By using the spiritual sense of touch, you will able to feel and discern things in the spiritual realm. And that is always amazing! Ask the Lord to expand and show you what you are feeling or sensing in your spirit.

Chapter 4

FEELING THE HEART OF GOD

~~~

Because you are one with Christ, you have the ability to literally feel the heart of God. For you beautiful "feelers" out there, it is the way you are wired. It's an emotional connection and sometimes, it can be overwhelming. You may wonder if what you feel is actually coming from you, God, or even another person. You may not know why you feel a certain emotion. Emotions such as grief or joy may suddenly sweep over you all. You may also be very empathetic, intuitively picking upon the way others feel. It's a heart connection through which God leads you. It can also function as a form of a word of knowledge. A word of knowledge is one of the gifts of the Spirit in 1 Corinthians 12:4-8, and is simply the Holy Spirit transmitting His specific knowledge to you about something that you would have no ability or means to be able to know on your own.

If you come into someone's presence and all of a sudden you feel fear, anger, lust, whatever... and you were fine before you did that, you are probably connecting to their atmosphere. Recognize this is not you. Your next step is to ask God why you're feeling this and what you should do about it.

Scripture says Jesus only did what He "saw" the Father doing (John 5:19). And, also, that Jesus was moved with compassion in certain situations. The compassion He felt drew Him to people (Matthew 20:34).

³⁴ Jesus was deeply moved with compassion toward them. So, he touched their eyes, and instantly they could see! Jesus said to them, "Your faith has healed you."

So, let me help you, if you are a "feeler." You are not crazy! Use what you are picking up. It bears repeating, ask God why you're feeling what you're feeling and what you should do about it. Sometimes He will have you minister to or pray for someone or simply encourage them. Sometimes, it is a private prayer project between you and Him. As an adjunct, when you feel emotions, you need to be careful not to project your emotions on others. Just because you feel something, others aren't necessarily feeling the same way. All this, like any other gift, requires practice, but practice pays off in glorious ways.

Often with this modality, it is used in conjunction with seeing or hearing modalities. I will take this opportunity to expound on how connecting with God works practically. Very often we are led to flow from one modality to the next. For me, I often get a simple picture/moving picture (I am a seer) and, as I focus on it, God expands it and gives me words/phrases. The more I focus on it, the more I get. However, sometimes, I will get a word/phrase first and then He will "speak" to me in pictures (moving or static). Often, I will feel God's heart on the matter and feel weightiness on my body. Occasionally I will get a fragrance or taste. There is a flow to it that works when we relax and let things unfold. Whatever you "get", linger there, and often you will get more. Don't be afraid to ask God questions. He LOVES engaging back and forth with His kids. This is your adventure with Him! And, when you cultivate engaging with Him when it is not life or death, then when the "heavy duty" issues come up, you are poised to be able to "hear" better!

All engagement is cultivated by intimacy and, when cultivated, can happen supernaturally in a way that feels very natural. You were made for connection with God!

Chapter 5

GOD THINKING THROUGH YOU

~~~

God can also communicate with you through your thoughts. He can literally think through your mind. Scripture says we have the "mind of Christ" (1 Corinthians 2:16). It is a Holy Spirit "mind meld" that we have access to, and like any other connection, can be cultivated through practice. You can tell when God is thinking through you, because the thought is intermingled with supernatural peace, joy, and empowerment. If you are wired to "hear" God in your thoughts, you may think, "God doesn't speak to me", because it can be difficult to discern which thoughts are yours and which are God's. I promise you that God HAS spoken to you before; He is a communicator, He is the WORD! You might not have recognized it as His voice, though. It takes practice to discern when God is thinking through you, but it is an exquisitely powerful way to receive from God.

My husband, Brian, is a thinker on steroids. This used to frustrate him to no end. Here was His prophetic wife getting visions and words and sensations in her body, and he would seek God and receive "nothing." But, my husband is exquisitely wired for God to think through him. When He realized this, He was freed and empowered to attend to what was coming through His mind. He started picking up on what God was showing him personally. This was and is usually accompanied by supernatural peace that causes his heart to rest.

Usually, thinkers get their "aha" moments after some internal or external processing. They're the ones that need to go away and chew on whatever they received. Thinkers, the more you grow in your discernment, the easier it will be to identify the thoughts that come from God. God-thoughts carry a greater weight and more peace than non-God-thoughts. Thoughts from God, as well as any other way we have connected to God, will always be in agreement with God's Word (rightly interpreted), His nature (other-giving Love, Truth, Peace), the finished work of Jesus, grace that supplies rather than demands, freedom, and edification (building up).

Chapter 6

KNOWING IN YOUR "KNOWER"

~~~

I am convinced that we have an organ in the spirit called our "knower." Some people "hear" the Lord through their "knower". They are led by "knowing." This is basically intuitive sensing. You just know. You don't know why you know, you just have an intuitive sense deep down. You know that you know! It may be subtle, but it's how you are led if you are a "knower".

This is how my husband and I knew we were to marry one another. Truly, we did not have a promising "profile" or track record for a good marriage (there's lots of story here for another time). But we just knew that we knew – weighty knowledge! As of this writing, we are entering 25 years of a great marriage. I am so grateful we followed our "knowers".

I have ministered to people who were soooo shut down that this was the only way they could connect to God at that time. But God used this deep knowing so powerfully - joy and freedom would come every time. That is gorgeous fruit!

So, allow yourself to quiet down and connect with what you know deep down. Don't invalidate or dismiss it! Guess Who's deep down in your knower? That's right - Holy Spirit! God loves to communicate to you through your "knower".

Chapter 7

BEING LED THROUGH SCRIPTURE

~~~

Scripture is designed to connect us with God and bring wisdom and guidance. The Word or originally "logos" in the Greek, is not the physical Bible, but the Person of Christ (John 1:1). Scripture is intended to point to Christ AS The Word. As it does, it is being used how God intended it to be used – to bring abundant life (John 10:10).

This is a crucial distinction because the Bible has been and can be misused. When we misinterpret or misapply Scripture, it does the exact opposite of giving life. It violates Love! Most of us have been "beaten up" with Scripture one time or another. Jesus lambasted against this (Matthew 23:13–39) and revealed that, when Scripture brings death, it is the result of the pharisaical Mosaic law and the religious spirit behind it. We are under law – just not that one. We are under the glorious law of Love (John 15:12-16), and freedom (James 1:25; 2:12; 2 Corinthians 3:17), and of the Spirit (Romans 8:2). If the Scripture you are reading makes you feel heavy, condemned, angry, or fearful, understand you are missing something in your interpretation. Simply put, Jesus is not like that (Matthew 11:28-20; 1 John 4:8, 16), and neither is Father God (Hebrews 1:3; John 14:7,9)! They are Love (1 John 4:8,16), so they are lovely! If you can't reconcile what you sense in your knower with what scripture appears to say, give your conflict to Jesus and let Him lead as/when He will. Rest. God is nothing but endlessly good. You are adored!

Scripture has universal application, but it also can speak to you very personally. As you read the Bible, ask Holy Spirit to speak to you. Many times, you will see a specific verse "jump out at you." This is God speaking to you! Or you may suddenly receive revelation about a verse and know how to apply it to your situation even though you've read it many times before without understanding. This is Holy Spirit highlighting the written word. This is a rhema word. Rhema is a Greek word used in the Bible for the instant, personal spoken word of God to us. Rhema (ῥῆμα in Greek) literally means an "utterance" or "thing said."

Holy Spirit can move through scripture to guide you very individually. You may be in a situation where you don't know what to do and out of nowhere a verse comes to mind that brings the solution. That is the Lord speaking a rhema word to you. Truly, the sons/daughters of God are led by the Spirit of God (Romans 8:14).

Be aware, as well, that just because you truly hear God speaking something personally to you, whether in Scripture or any other way, does not mean that it is automatically for everyone else. God is very personal and individual with the leading of His kids. What brings life to you at this time may not do so for someone else. Be sensitive, humble, and led by Love!

Chapter 8

BEING LED THROUGH SUPERNATURAL SIGNS

~~~

Despite being careful stewards of what God shares with us, we don't want to limit God. He can highlight or draw attention and bring revelation or confirmation through anything. He would not be a relational God if He only spoke through the letters of The Bible, as authoritative and inspired as it is. He is limitless and exuberant in His desire for connection with His kids.

He can even and often does lead us through ungodly things and people who have set themselves up as His enemy (although He is the enemy of no one, Colossians 1:21). We see this with ungodly kings, prophets and leaders, who actually spoke truth. We see this all the time in so-called "secular" venues. For example, God speaks through movies all the time that are totally non-Christian movies. He will speak through industries that are all about making money or through politics. The tearing down of pagan dualism (the separation of the spiritual and natural) is pertinent here, but a complex discussion for another time. Suffice it to say, there is nowhere in God's creation that God is not. Everyone and everything can be holy, even if blinded and in disguise!

God also communicates with signs that speak to you, but make you wonder! Signs point to things. God speaks through signs that point to Himself. And there are limitless ways He speaks in this way!

I had a period when I had been giving and serving in ministry for years, but at the time I felt invisible and utterly drained. I was past frustrated and had experienced intense loss. Tears flowed down my face as I was driving down the pass from where I had been ministering and, suddenly, through the clouds the sun burst forth and a rainbow appeared and inexplicably landed on my car hood. It remained there for a full 20 minutes as the love, glory, and favor of God spoke to me over and over, "You're seen...you're favored...you're loved!" It ministered to my heart powerfully without words!

A word of caution: We need to make sure our perspective of God is whole, loving, and redemptive. Otherwise, we'll perceive natural disasters, epi/pandemics, and trials as God's judgment. We will filter tragedy through the wrath of God. These interpretations of natural phenomena and consequences are not consistent with God as Love, Who sacrifices Himself and does not demand sacrifice. They are not consistent with a God, Who truly has forgiven and forgotten our sin (Psalms 103:12, Isaiah 43:5, Hebrews 8:12; 10:17). He is endlessly merciful and gracious. This is often us projecting our fears, alienation, brokenness, and unloveliness on a God, Who has never been against His kids (Jeremiah 32:35, Matthew 23:37...), nor condemns them (Romans 8:1, John 3:17). He saves in every sense of the word! When we see God as other-giving Love, Who is utterly good, we see Him as He truly is and can discern more accurately how He is moving.

In addition, I recommend using this mode of receiving as confirmation only when making big life decisions. Oftentimes we can read into things what we ardently desire and be misled. I also do not recommend "throwing out fleeces" (Judges 6:36–40). That would be something like, "If I am to marry so and so, God, have a green truck drive by followed by a bicycle." That is not relational and can really mislead and confuse. Disastrous results can ensue, leaving you angry at God when it was not Him at all! This brings us to our next all-important discussion.

Chapter 9

HOW TO KNOW WHEN YOU ARE HEARING GOD

~~~

So how do you know if what we hear is from God, the devil (however you interpret him/it) or just yourself? If it's devilish, it won't be in line with love. It will lack peace and not be scripturally accurate (interpreted rightly). Both the voices of the devil and self tend to be accusatory and condemning. When it's from self (referred to as the "carnal mind" or the "flesh", Romans 8:6-11), it will be contrary to the Spirit of God and often birthed out of our own selfish motives.

⁷ In fact, the mind-set focused on the flesh fights God's plan and refuses to submit to his direction, because it cannot! Romans 8:7 (TPT)

When a message is from God, it will carry the fruit of the Spirit (Galatians 5:22-23). It will bear the fruit of love – our command! It will bring joy, peace, patience, kindness, goodness, faithfulness, and self-control - not controlling others. It will not cause fear or anxiety (1 John 4:18). It will not condemn (Romans 8:1). It will bring freedom (James 1:25; 2:12; 2 Corinthians 3:17). It will always line up with scripture, rightly interpreted. For more on that, you can go to my four-part blog series, "How to Handle Scripture Rightly" at catherinetoon.com.

Every time you get something that you think is from the Lord, filter it through the Word of God, the finished work of Jesus, and the character of God. Is it in line with His nature? Remember that God is Love and nothing He says will ever violate that (John 4:8,16).

Anything from God will carry peace in the inmost parts of your being – the place where you're one with Christ. The Word says to let peace be the umpire of your heart, sifting and deciding all things. God will always reliably lead you through peace (Colossians 3:15, AMPC)!

[15]And let the peace (soul harmony which comes) from Christ rule (act as umpire continually) in your hearts [deciding and settling with finality all questions that arise in your minds, in that peaceful state] to which as [members of Christ's] one body you were also called [to live]. And be thankful (appreciative), [giving praise to God always]. (Emphasis added)

If it is from God, there is a settling in your spirit (in your "knower"), and in that peaceful place, confusion goes (1 Corinthians 14:33, KJV):

[33]For God is not the author of confusion, but of peace, as in all churches of the saints.

That peace will grow the more you sit with it. Moreover, the Word of God says that the sons of God are led by the Spirit of God (Romans 8:14, KJV).

For as many as are led by the Spirit of God, they are the sons of God.

Sometimes, if you think what you are getting is from God, but you're not 100% sure, it's helpful to sit with it. If it is indeed from God, He will continue to convince you. Peace will grow the more you sit with it or move in that direction. If it's not from Him, you will lose peace. Follow peace at all costs! I will say it again, do not violate your peace! That is Holy Spirit leading you. You can bank your life on it!

Chapter 10

WHAT DOES LOVE LOOK LIKE?

~~~

When God communicates, it always tastes, smells, sounds, looks like and feels like love because God is love. Love is always kind to you. Love is always patient with you and always uplifting. Love will always encourage you. Love delights in you and always believes the best about you. If what you are getting doesn't feel like love, it's not from God. He cannot operate outside of Who He is. Love is righteous and pure, so He will never instruct you to do something immoral or dishonest. Love will never condemn you or beat you down. When you're in the presence of Love, you feel safe, empowered, energized, and cherished.

Chapter 11

SUBMITTING WHAT YOU'RE GETTING

~~~

It is also helpful, especially when you're first starting to practice "hearing" God, to share what you receive with mature people in your life. There are many people in the Body of Christ who have matured in their ability to connect with God and can help you navigate the spiritual revelation you get. Make sure these people are mature in the Word and in things of the Spirit. Make sure that you have a sense that these people genuinely care for you. Proverbs 11:14 tells us that in the multitude of counselors there is safety.

But, with that, understand you have your OWN personal relationship with God. You are one with Him – He is inside of you and wildly cares about you. So, if the word passes through all the safeguards and it is full of peace and life-giving, do not let anyone talk you out of it! At the end of the day, this is you and God!

Chapter 12

PRACTICING CONNECTING WITH GOD

~~~

Just having knowledge of your five spiritual senses and other means of connecting with God is not the same as experiencing Him in fullness. Your ability to connect with Him experientially can, and ideally should, be cultivated and developed by practice and use (Hebrews 5:13-14, TPT):

¹³ For every spiritual infant who lives on milk is not yet pierced by the revelation of righteousness. 14 But solid food is for the mature, whose spiritual senses perceive heavenly matters. And they have been adequately trained by what they've experienced to emerge with understanding of the difference between what is truly excellent and what is evil and harmful.

Begin to practice connecting with God on a regular basis. Every time you use your spiritual senses, they will grow and develop. I like to practice my connection with God by having him help me in smaller details, like picking out melons. That way, if I "blow it", it's just a bum melon! He cares about all the details of your life.

If you care about it, God cares about it. Such exercises will cause you will to hone in your discernment to know if what you're getting is from you, "the devil", or God. Practice His presence regularly. He wants you to enjoy your day with Him. That makes every day a happy holy day!

There are so many ways to connect to God and they're ALL available to you. Start with the way you "hear" God the best, and really practice that. Hone it, don't despise it. Value your ability to connect with Him in your way and practice, practice, practice. Focus is powerful. Remember, God didn't give you defunct spiritual equipment. He gave you all the equipment you need! The more you practice, the more experienced and better you will get. As you develop connecting with God in one way, other ways will likely open up. Ask Him for these. It's thrilling to connect with God in new and greater ways! Religion may be boring, but God is never boring!

Chapter 13

GROWING IN YOUR CONNECTION

~~~

If you're just starting out, you'll need to give yourself some dedicated time to grow in your ability to connect with God. One thing that is really helpful as you practice is asking God questions about what He's trying to show you. It can be very practical. The supernatural is not always spectacular. Sometimes it's subtle.

Journaling can be very helpful as you learn to connect with God, because it causes you to focus. Simply write down a question you have for the Lord, and then write whatever comes to you. Relax! Don't critique what you are getting. Many times what you are writing will truly be from God – especially if it is really really good!

Trust Holy Spirit to help you – He is the Helper. It's His job and He loves it! He wants you to experience heaven on earth right now, right where you are. He wants that intimacy with you more than you want it. He wants you to have the answers that you need even more than you want them. All of that comes from a place of connection with Him. Jesus said that the Holy Spirit will lead us and guide us into all truth (John 16:13). He is trustworthy and will not lead you down the wrong path. Get to know Him and develop your friendship with Him. He is so wild about you!

Chapter 14

IT'S OK TO MISS IT

~~~

Relax! Connecting with God is about practice not perfection. It is OK to miss it! God is about relationship with you, not about your performance. I don't get it right all the time. But I have found the more I relax and put the "onus" on God, the more I get and the less I "miss it"! But, of course, I still "miss it" at times!

I remember one time, I was driving in a town I am not familiar with. I was talking to one of my friends, who I really admired, who was in a different car, and we were trying to find a restaurant. He suggested that we "follow the Spirit" to the restaurant. He said he'd follow my lead. Well, needless to say, we ended up on a dirt road in a blind alley. Hahaha! It was at that time I "felt led" to use Google Maps! Praise God we got there and we both had a great laugh! I suspect no one laughed harder than Holy Spirit!

God is absolutely delighted with you and enjoys the process. He will never criticize you when you miss it! Just like when a little toddler is learning to walk, we don't condemn them when they fall down; we celebrate that they tried and maybe took a few steps! Your Father is the same way, He delights to see you growing and cheers you on for trying. He's a loving, tender Father. He sees your heart and just adores you. Bask in His delight with you every step of the way. See Him smiling at you and cherishing every moment with you. He rejoices over you (Zephaniah 3:17, NKJV)!

[17] The Lord your God in your midst, The Mighty One, will save; He will rejoice over you with gladness, He will quiet you with His love, He will rejoice over you with singing."

Since this all about practice, you can get tons of practice using your spiritual equipment from my book, Marked by Love, Unveiling the Substance of Your True Identity. You can go Amazon to get your copy. I also have a workbook by the same name, if that works better for you. However you go about it, be intentional. Your spiritual life and life in general will come alive!

Chapter 15

IMPARTATION

~~~

Let me pray over you!

Papa,

I thank You for Your heart to connect intimately with Your adored kids! I thank You that none are disqualified, or have defunct spiritual equipment! If there are any lies here that need ministry, which would hinder your son/daughter from connecting with You, I thank You for releasing Your love, truth and freedom in palpable ways to your son/daughter right in that place!

In the name in Jesus, I speak to eyes, ears, hearts, and minds, to be opened and made alive to enjoy and be enjoyed by Papa/Jesus/ Holy Spirit! I thank You that You are always safe, and life-giving! Minister to Your treasured son/daughter in whatever ways they need!
I thank You for massive upgrades in experiential connection with You!

In Jesus' name – amen!

Wow! I am soooo excited for you! I'd love to hear from you about your new experiences – whohoo!

Love,

Catherine

ABOUT CATHERINE

~~~

As an MD in residency, Catherine's life was radically transformed when she encountered the real Jesus, who walked her out of years of heavy bondage. In the process, He birthed a deep compassion in her to reach out to others with the love and power of a wildly passionate God who heals, transforms, restores the broken, oppressed and infirm and releases them into powerful destinies.

After 4 years practicing as a board-certified Internist, she retired from medicine to raise her children and wholeheartedly pursue God's call on her life. She has ministered tirelessly in numerous capacities including prayer, healing, prophetic coaching, sozo, wholeness coaching, training, teaching, preaching and equipping. She directed healing rooms, The Transformation Center, Encounter Ministries, and ran conferences. She also served on the Senior Leadership team of Prayer Mountain, as well as its board. In addition, she was the Director of the Emerge Campus School of Transformation. Catherine was ordained as an Apostle and Prophet in February of 2015 and served as an Instructor at World

Bible School University. She also serves on the board of The Safe Place. Catherine is an anointed author and speaker. Her prophetic voice has proven  to be repeatedly accurate in speaking forth vision, direction, confirmation, and practical strategic insight into individuals, leaders, and organizations around the globe.

In 2016, she founded Imprint, LLC, later followed by Catherine Toon Ministries. Both entities are dedicated to restoring wholeness, revealing identity, and releasing destiny through the unveiling of God's imprint of Love uniquely expressed in every person. In 2017, she released her first book, Marked by Love, which takes the reader on a wild encounter with God as Love to discover their true identity through the lens of the imprint placed upon every person by God, the lover of our souls. Because of the book's wonderful reception, she followed up with a Marked by Love online course, workbook, leaders' guide, Rare and Beautiful Treasures mini-book, and How to Hear God, An Experiential Journey with more books to come. She is a sought-out speaker, and coach and resides with her husband and her 3 powerhouse children in Colorado.

For more information about Catherine Toon and Imprint, see www.catherinetoon.com.

SHARE YOUR TESTIMONY

~~~

Send me a note at: info@catherinetoon.com

CONNECT WITH CATHERINE

~~~

Receive weekly prophetic words, blogs, and more direct to your inbox.

Sign up @ https://catherinetoon.com

FOLLOW

~~~

▮	Facebook	@CatherineToonMD
◉	Instagram	@catherinetoon
▶	YouTube	@Catherine Toon, MD
🐦	Twitter	@CatherineToonMD
in	LinkedIn	@Catherine Toon
℗	Pinterest	@ CatherineToonMD

REQUEST

~~~

If you would like Catherine to speak at your event or more intimate gathering, contact us at:

https://catherinetoon.com/request/ or info@catherinetoon.com

RESOURCES

~~~

Catherine's Blog go to:

https://catherinetoon.com/blog/

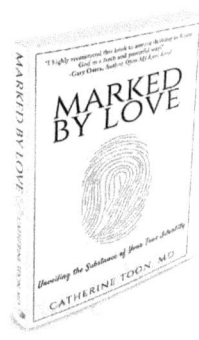

Marked by Love – the Book
in paperback, Kindle,
and Audible on Amazon

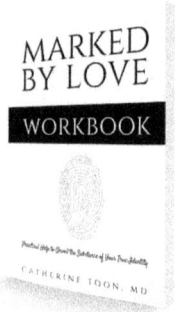

Marked by Love – the Workbook
in paperback on Amazon

Marked by Love – Leader's Guide
in paperback on Amazon

**Marked by Love
Online Course** go to
catherinetoon.com

Rare and Beautiful Treasures Mini-book
in paperback on Amazon or download
for free at: https://catherinetoon.com

Journey with Jesus Activation
download for free at:
https://catherinetoon.com